LIFEMATES
SERIES

A Busy Man's Guide to Romancing His Wife

Mike Keyes

Love. Honor. Cherish.
faithmarriage.com

Faith Marriage is an imprint of Cook Communications
Ministries, Colorado Springs, Colorado 80918
Cook Communications, Paris, Ontario
Kingsway Communications, Eastbourne, England

THEY CALL ME MR. ROMANCE
© 2001 by Vincent Michael Keyes III

First Printing, 2001
Printed in the United States of America

1 2 3 4 5 6 7 8 9 10 Printing/Year 05 04 03 02 01

Editor: Craig Bubeck, Sr. Editor
Design: Image Studios
Photograph: Gene Photography

Library of Congress Cataloging-in-Publication Data
Applied for
ISBN 0781436915

Table of Contents

Every professional coach needs to read the *Mr. Romance* wake up call! I found myself laughing and crying; not only with Mike, but for myself as well. Thanks Mike!

—Jim Montrella
former swimming coach Ohio State, USC, and
the 1976 U.S. Olympic Swim Team

Mike has laid bare the wounds of the ladder of success. His honest recognition of the hard work it takes to keep your priorities in order has had an impact on me. It made me want to grab my wife and head for a bed and breakfast, or Hawaii. In fact, I did!

—Kenneth Davis
Vice President, Operations, Interdent

For those of us who like to think we have the world by the tail (but deep down know better), Mike's story is sure to hit home. This man has done everything to the extreme; and once you start reading his book, you'll want to read it cover to cover in one sitting, just as I did.

—Donald J. DiCostanzo
President, Wynn Oil Company

Romance has never been said so profoundly! Mike has give me at least ten powerful, practical ideas for loving my wife in the real world. He thinks like men think: "bottom line, give it to me straight."

—Doug Slaybaugh
Executive Director, Purpose Driven

Preface

This wasn't my idea.

I don't have the type of life that you write books about. Fact is, I enjoy reading about others and their ideas. I never thought anyone would want to read about mine.

Then one night I was lying in bed, and I realized that I was closer to the end of my life than the beginning of it. Maybe I did have something to share. Life sure looks different from the back nine.

So I decided to listen to my friends and offer for your consideration a few stories from a rather not-so-quiet existence. My friends seem to think that I have a lot of energy, and maybe I do. My friends also seem to think that I move around my life like a bull in a china shop.

Okay, I do.

And my friends seem to think that some of the decisions I have made over the last 16 years of my marriage have built an unusual and surprisingly strong relationship with my wife, in a marriage few thought could last. They want me to be honest and real—to let you see how a marriage can be built, one brick at a time, even by the kind of guy who would rather close a deal than buy flowers for his wife.

People take risks with a book like this. People like Craig Bubeck, who cashed in a few chips getting this book through the way I wrote it. And Cook Communications deserves a slap on the back for putting their seal of approval on this project. Mike Yorkey was a nice guy to take some time to make sure all my sentences had verbs in them.

I'm sure my mom and dad never thought their son would write a book, much less one about marriage. What they may not understand is that I made it because of some of the things they did right.

My undying gratitude goes to Lisa's parents, Jim and Joyce—their relationship, more than any other I have encountered, bore the fruit that I so sincerely desired for my own life. I want our marriage to be a gift to them.

There are a few special guys who knew me when and still stuck with me through the changes: Randy Babcook, Tom Ketchum, Tony Robbins, Dan Marshall, Doug Carpenter, Chris Tooker, Rick McCarthy, Ken Davis, and my "shiny" friend, Bob Unvert.

Doug Slaybaugh, Brian Thatcher, the men of Beyond the Bottom Line (BBL), and Dave and Jan Congo—you have all been my plumb line. You'll never know all the times you kept me on track.

Thom Black—look what you got me into! Thanks for your friendship and for putting a heartbeat to my stories. This would have never happened without you.

My daughters, a.k.a. Scooter and Sparky, may wonder how all this could be true. What they will never wonder about is how much their daddy loves their mom.

And of course, my bride Lisa Keyes—it may say CEO on my business card, but you are the COO of the household and the MVP of my life. Thanks for not letting me forget that true success has a lot more to do with who we are than with what we accomplish.

And finally to you, the reader—turn your cell phone off and come on in.

We need to have a talk.

Introduction

They call me Mr. Romance . . .

I don't know what they call me behind my back.

You probably don't care much about who I am. What's more important is that you care what I am.

I am a stubborn, tough son-of-a-gun. I like John Wayne movies. I play with pain. I get my way a lot—probably too much. I've smoked big cigars and swaggered out of more bars in the wee hours of the morning with big deals stuck in my back pocket than I care to remember.

I have lost more money than most people ever make, and there was a time when I thought I knew and had it all.

I have also been married to Lisa now for almost two decades, and frankly it's amazing my marriage has stayed together. For most of the time I'd been way too busy to even think about it—too busy to build a relationship, too busy to romance my wife, too busy to care.

Maybe you're where I was. You never stop being busy, but somewhere along the line, you wake up to the fact that someone very precious may be slipping out of your life. If you are lucky, you wake up in time.

I loved Lisa too much to lose her just because I was being stupid. Romance wasn't exactly my game. But I had to learn.

I know that I haven't been the best husband in the world. There are a whole bunch of women who would throw me into the ocean if they had a chance. I'm sure Lisa will get letters from wives asking her how she puts up with me. That's okay. Let them write.

I have only one woman in the world that I have to be concerned about. And as long as she is happy, then my world is in pretty good shape.

That's why they call me Mr. Romance, and what you're about to read are my stories.

They're all true.

My Days as Mr. Big Shot

CHAPTER ONE

Let me start by telling you about one of the most difficult experiences of my life. It changed the way I think, even to this day.

Over twenty years ago, I started a commercial real estate business in Orange County, California. I was one of the early realtors to work with clients who had real estate needs around the United States. Life was great. I would sign up a client who needed to lease or sell real estate in multiple locations across the country. This meant I could develop long-term relationships with my clients instead of working on a single property, only to move on when the deal was done. I was traveling a lot—too much—but I enjoyed meeting people from different cities. Little did I know how negatively that was affecting my life at home.

I took my clients seriously. I would do almost anything for a client. Too many people are looking on to their next deal before they complete the one they are on. That's idiotic! You have to take care of the girl you brought to the dance. That is what I do, and I am really good at it. I make my client feel as though he is my life.

And I'll tell you; my lifestyle was proof of my success. I was making big money. I would make in one deal what some people made in a year. When you get on a roll like that and the money comes so easily, it affects you in funny ways. To impress my wife (or maybe I was impressing myself), I walked into a Mercedes dealer one day and bought her a sedan without even asking her whether she wanted one. A few weeks later, I saw a Jeep that I liked. You never know when you will need a third car! I wanted it that day, so I bought it—with my credit card. I thought everyone put cars on their credit card. The people I was moving with certainly did.

Everything was working well because I was doing what I said I would do. I thought I had everything covered. It's a trust game. Keep your promises and the clients keep coming back.

I had a particular client I was representing who became my biggest single source of income. I was bringing home over $500,000 a year from real estate deals with him. He trusted me to arrange real estate purchases for his company around the country. I would fly around and secure the contracts, sometimes even signing for them while the paperwork was being completed. I trusted him as much as he trusted me.

Then he betrayed me—he wasn't square with me. After five years of representing this client by making commitments to landlords, I suddenly found this guy was in the middle of filing for bankruptcy. I can't even imagine what he was thinking. He never gave me a clue that this was going on.

To appreciate what was going on, you have to understand what happens in a real estate transaction. If I'd begun to work a deal with a landlord for a property, he would stop showing that property. Sometimes he'd even start to develop it for me, investing thousands of dollars of improvements for me to move in my clients. People so trusted me that they would pull property off the market just because I said so. They would start improving an office space, spending a lot of money to fix it up, just because I said so. As I said, people trusted me to get the deal closed.

The problem was, now the company I represented—my largest client—was about to go bankrupt. And the dude hadn't told me a thing. I had contracts and properties all over the country that I had negotiated on behalf of this client, and he no longer intended to honor those contracts. Even though he could fulfill his obligation on those properties, he was going bankrupt!

But . . . it was *my* phone that started ringing: "I thought this was a done deal, Mike. We trusted, you, Mike. We turned down other offers because of you, Mike. We already have thousands of dollars of improvements into the property. We trusted you, Mike."

The best time of my life became the worst time of my life. I knew I had to take care of every single one of these people who had depended on me. In the meantime, my client bankrupted his business and moved to Oklahoma. I was left alone to figure out his mess.

Hundreds of thousands of dollars were owed. My biggest income source was gone. I started borrowing money to honor commitments made on my name. I plunged into a personal hell.

What made it really bad was the sense that I was disappointing my family. I couldn't even buy Christmas presents for my wife and kids. I had gone from a substantial provider to what I considered a bum, all in a matter of days.

There are no silver linings in moments like that. You work through them and see what you have when you are finished. Time passed, and I emerged with my honor intact. And I regained people's trust. But here's the really amazing thing—I also gained an understanding for the first time of what romance is about.

I had a lot of quiet moments over those several months. The only voice that touched me was the voice of my wife. She soothed me. She encouraged me. She forced me to make choices about her that I had never made.

I had to decide who she was to me. Was she my ally or my enemy? Would I bring her into my world or build a wall between her and me? Would I give her a voice or silence her?

For me, these were tough, tough decisions. I was used to doing everything myself, and I despised weakness. But I decided to let her in.

I decided Lisa was the most important partner I had. Later I would come to realize that I was so concerned about trusting others and having others trust me, that I had failed to build that into this part of our relationship. I usually concealed things from her. I didn't share things about the business and my work. I kept financial dealings away from home. I just brought home checks.

Understand that this isn't easy for me to say, but . . . I was wrong. If you're like I was, you probably think romancing your wife means ordering in pizza followed by 10 minutes of sex. But the truth is real romance means making her a partner. It means sharing your life with her.

When I began the difficult and new experience of sharing everything with her, I had to get used to her responses. I couldn't control what she might say or think. But that was okay. My gut told me this was someone I could really trust.

I think the hardest thing was to give her control. I made myself listen to her. Sometimes she was more right than I. She deserved to have a voice. I had never allowed her one.

A busy man overlooks thousands of opportunities to romance his wife. I have. You will. We can't afford to. Romance can't happen if you don't make a decision to treasure your wife and make her a part of your life . . . both the good and the bad of it.

My Work Is a Roaring Lion

CHAPTER TWO

Someone asked me whom this book was for.

I asked him what he did. He said he drove a truck.

I love truck drivers, but this book probably isn't for your typical truck drivers. That's because most guys I know who drive trucks do it mostly just to make a living. They can't wait for the day to end. There are a lot of places they would rather be than driving a truck.

That's not my life.

My job consumes me.

It's the first thing I am thinking about when I wake up and the last thing I am thinking about when I finally go to sleep.

For me, a forty-hour workweek seems like a vacation. I schedule appointments before the kids are out of bed in the morning, and I eat dinner with clients when my wife is climbing in bed at night. I have had to call home from out of town because I wanted to know how a teacher-parent conference went while I was on the road.

So I'm not exaggerating when I say, my work is a roaring lion that constantly threatens to consume me.

It distorts my values and my priorities.

It seduces me and wants all of me.

Sometimes I wish I had a job I could hate—a job where I could watch the clock, waiting for 5:00 o'clock to come so I could run for the car and leave all this until tomorrow. I'd wish I had the freedom to have the clarity of mind to focus all my energy on my wife and my kids and the things that were important to me.

But I don't have that kind of job.

I love my work.

So the battle within me rages on. How will I direct myself today between my two loves— between the busyness of my work and the romancing of my wife? What decisions will I make today that will show me to be a man who is in control of his life?

The way I've come to see it—each day is my Super Bowl, and I am only as good as my last play.

Dancing with the Devil

You have to be careful of the people with whom you choose to work. People have a tendency to rub off on each other, and it seems like it's more the bad stuff that rubs off than the good.

If it's in your heart to romance your wife, then you have to realize that some of these relationships can be deadly.

I had a client a few years back, a middle-age guy, who was on the way up . . . big time on the way up. I met him when he had one employee, and I was with him until he had 3,000 employees. That's a big show.

To put it delicately, he wasn't one of the good guys. He was tough. He used his money—and he had a lot of it—to buy everything. He had to. He was arrogant, prideful, and in my opinion, just plain revolting. I think he would have eaten alone if he didn't tie money around his neck.

He was the meanest and the most disrespectful man I had ever worked with. He cursed out his employees in front of other people, screamed at people, and treated everyone like scum.

This guy was my client. I stood to make a whole lot of money off him. I just had to do one thing. I had to play his game.

So I did. I lowered myself to be a part of his life. I wanted his business so much that I included myself in this guy's circle. And I never said a word—for years.

One time I was closing a real estate deal for this guy in Chicago. The landlord was a wonderful man who lived in Germany, and my client wanted to lease three floors of his building. The landlord flew all the way from Europe to close the deal because he wanted to meet my client and me. I had talked to him on the phone, and I was touched by how kind he seemed. It's unusual for a landlord to invest so much personal contact time into a lessee.

My client showed up for the meeting—late, hung over from the night before, and sweating like a pig even though it was a freezing Chicago winter. He walked into the room, where I was already talking with our German landlord, and started to tear the man apart. He told him that his building was a piece of garbage. He screamed at him, claiming what an awful deal the lease was and how he would never sign such a bad contract. He wound up stomping out and leaving me to pick up the pieces.

But I still never said anything.

I wanted the next deal.

The thing is, I was becoming like him because I wasn't walking away.

My wife couldn't tolerate him. Lisa thought he was bad for me. She kept telling me to let loose, but I wouldn't. She told me to do the deal and get away. Eventually the friction between Lisa and me over this client became intense.

I thought I was being a good husband, making decisions that kept the money coming in. And I was busy. Can't make money if you aren't busy. But I was making real romance impossible. I was destroying the atmosphere in our home where romance is seeded.

Looking back, I can see how I was almost becoming like this guy. I was becoming hard and insensitive. I was becoming short-tempered and mean. I would actually walk out of a meeting with this guy, pick up the phone to talk to my wife, and be just as mean to her as he had just been to an employee. I couldn't turn myself on and off like a faucet, and the stream of abuse was beginning to flow just as easily from me.

It might sound cliché, but I'm telling you—you can't have romance in your marriage when you are selling your soul to the devil.

So I stopped dealing with this client, and he went away. Just like that.

And as hard as the loss of business was, the gain in my marriage was almost immediate.

Romance is not a single act. It is a state of mind that is reinforced by a lifetime of decisions. There is no way I could cultivate a romantic relationship with my wife and tolerate the horrible abuses this man generated every day of his life.

Looking back now, there's no way I'd put up with a guy who treated people like my client did.

But you see, business is funny that way. It can compromise you one deal at a time if you aren't careful. First you lose your principles, and before you know it you've lost your marriage.

The kind of sensitivity I'm talking about is the bedrock of real romance, just like it is in business. After all, if I don't care what my wife thinks, how can I care what my customers and clients think?

The Art
of Persuasion

CHAPTER FOUR

I am a friend to a number of professional athletes. There's something I've noticed about them all—the reason they are pros is because they do one thing very, very well.

I also know many guys like me who have successful businesses. We too do one thing very well. That's basic to our success.

It's easy to build a business or become a professional athlete with the one thing you do well. It's much harder to build a romantic relationship using the same ability.

I hate it when people call me a salesman. I don't sell. I persuade. I persuade people to change their minds. I convince people. I persuade people to buy. The tools I work with are the very edges of truth.

I'll grant you I've been known to stretch it a bit. There

have been times when, after I've finished with it, it may not have looked much like the truth anymore. But I liked to always think it was in there somewhere. I'll admit that I can arrange the truth to serve me.

My point is, I can't turn it off. I am always persuading.

I had a client once named Rocky. He was a difficult client. I would never have provided him a facility in any building I owned. But he was my client. So I sold him to somebody else.

I persuaded landlords that this guy was the best tenant in the world. But he wasn't. I oversold what few good points the guy had. I would go in and get unbelievable concessions from the landlord to get this guy in the building, and I'd walk out laughing because of what I had done. Rocky always paid his rent, but man was he ever a pain in the owner's side throughout the entire term of the lease.

To me, it was all about winning. It was all about money. It was a game.

Then I would come home. For me, the game didn't stop. It was still about winning . . . and stretching the truth, whatever the issue: why I couldn't be home for dinner—why I needed to be late for a family obligation.

I was always stretching the truth, just like at work—always needing to win, just like at work.

The trouble was, Lisa was not playing a game. She wanted a relationship. She wanted raw truth, not the stretched-out kind. I was playing at home like I was playing at work, and it wasn't flying.

I had a pretty messed up view of romance. I saw it more like buying a hall pass. Take her out on a Friday or Saturday date, and Sunday golf or "Monday Night Football" was mine to do with as I pleased.

I basically had to learn how to turn myself off. It wasn't about winning and money at home. It was about trust and honesty and commitment. Real romance sprouts from a moment where you have honored your wife by withholding your need to persuade her; instead, you listen to what she needs. Real romance leaps from hallway conversations that are honest, and real, and softly spoken.

The funny thing is, in the end those were the important values in my work, too. In fact, I've come to realize that I need to be more at work like I am at home, rather than the other way around.

The Precious Commodity of Time

CHAPTER FIVE

Busy men have busy schedules. I have appointments to keep and people to manage. I spend and direct money—a lot of it. I can't call in sick today, or any day for that matter. If I'm gone for a day, the company loses two. Each hour I have is precious. I try to invest them like the valuable commodities they are.

So when I woke up and found myself coaching my five-year-old daughter's soccer team, I was sure that this was one massive mistake. I had never even played soccer. I was a tough guy on a college football team—240 pounds of angry nose guard. What was I doing coaching little girls' soccer? . . . especially one called the Rainbows!

I think Lindsay wondered what she was doing there as well. As the youngest one on the team, she had a hard time keeping up with the older girls. They were bigger and tougher. She wanted to quit. All I could say to her were my old football clichés.

"Honey, when the going gets tough, the tough get going."

"Come on, sweetheart! No pain, no gain."

"Winning isn't everything. It's the only thing."

Pretty bad stuff—didn't work at all. As the season dragged on, she got more upset. I talked her into hanging on through the last game. After that, she could do whatever she wanted to do in sports. I just didn't want her to quit.

Lisa was concerned that I was being too tough on her. She knew Lindsay was unhappy. She came to the games and seldom saw Lindsay have a chance to even kick the ball. Lindsay usually stood isolated by herself, running up and down the field away from the real action.

Lisa felt I needed to pay more attention to what Lindsay wanted instead of what I wanted. I think I heard that, but I still wanted it my way.

On the morning of the last game, Lindsay and I were driving to the game when I felt her looking at me with big tears in her eyes.

"I'm so sorry dad. I wish I had been better."

I slowed down and looked over at my daughter. I'm a pretty big guy, and next to me she is just a little tiny thing. But I realized in an instant that Lisa had been right. This wasn't a big deal I was trying to close. My daughter wasn't a building I was trying to unload. She was fragile and soft, and I was crushing her under the weight of my expectations.

I pulled the car off to the side of the road and squeezed her over into my arms. I told her how proud of her I was and how much I respected her. I could feel the wetness of her tears as I pressed her against my side. I found myself praying out loud to God, thanking Him for such a marvelous daughter as well as asking Him to give this precious child the courage to get through one more game.

That last game was a struggle. Against the best team in the league, we held our own until the very end. The Lollipops were as tough as their name suggested. And all the while, Lindsay stayed true to herself, running mightily up and down the field, fighting exhaustion. I'm sure she was just praying for the nightmare to end.

With just a few minutes remaining in the game, the goalie cleared the ball into a group of girls. A massive swarm of arms and legs fell upon the ball, and quietly—almost as if it were on a string—the ball popped out from the group and rolled toward Lindsay. Standing all by herself in front of the goalie, she stepped forward and softly kicked it into the corner of the net.

 Forever, as long as I live, I will always be able to close my eyes and see two visions from those next few moments. The first is Lindsay, running toward me with her hands raised over her head like an Olympic decathlon champion, dashing toward me as fast as a five-year-old can run, and screaming as loud as she could. I ran out to grab her, swallowing her up into my arms, roaring as if we had just won the World Cup.

And the second beautiful vision happened as I swung around with Lindsay in my arms. My eyes found Lisa in the bleachers, standing, cheering, and clapping as she watched us embrace. Forever I'll see her, tears running down her cheeks, mouthing to me the words: "I love you."

Romance is a funny thing. Sometimes it comes wrapped up in a box of chocolates or a bouquet of flowers. And sometimes it catches you by surprise as you sit on the sidelines watching your husband love your child.

It's important to my wife for me to be in love with our kids, and for our kids to be in love with me. My daughters are reflections of my wife's soul. She pours her life into them. When I love them, I love her.

There are lots of ways I can try to romance my wife. Who would have thought that loving her children would be one of them?

Approaching the Speed of Sound

CHAPTER SIX

Life speeds up a little at a time. It's like a black hole that sucks you in. One success after another, and you begin to approach terminal velocity. You can hardly go any faster. Your life becomes a blur.

I was thirty-seven when I hit terminal velocity. I had arrived at the pinnacle of my career. Life to me was seamless, and romance . . . well, I was going morning, noon, and night. It was breathtaking, and I wasn't about to stop to take one.

I was heading back to the office after a boy's afternoon out. It was 7:30 p.m., and I was cruising down the Pacific Coast Highway with the top down, the music blaring, and the phone in my ear. I was arguing with my wife, though, making excuses why I was to be late for dinner again. I don't think I was making much sense. After a five-hour lunch with clients and plenty of adult beverages, I wasn't thinking too clearly.

Something didn't feel right, and I looked in my mirror and saw flashing lights moving up right behind me. I slammed the phone down on the seat and pulled over. I was scared. I knew I was way over the legal limit in a number of areas.

I looked back, and the police officer was approaching my car with his gun drawn. He was yelling for me to get out with my hands up. I stepped out onto the road and looked down the barrel of his pistol. "Hands behind the head. Up against the car!" the police officer shouted in a firm voice. "Do you know how reckless you were driving? Are you crazy?"

The cop started to put me through the sobriety tests. Keep in mind I have these down cold. The walking test and the alphabet test. I used to practice them after half a dozen drinks so I could do them if I was stone drunk. But it didn't matter here. I was still going to get nailed by this officer.

All of a sudden the cop's radio goes nuts—an emergency call, and he has to move out right away. He slammed his hand against the hood of my car and screamed at me that I'm one lucky son of a gun and ran back to his car and squealed off down the road. I started to shake as I climbed back behind the wheel. That was too close!

I called Lisa, and we started to fight again. I wanted her to feel sorry for me because I was so scared. She was still mad about everything that was wrong with me and about us. I remember it was a long, lonely ride home.

It got worse. By the time I pulled into the garage, she came out to meet me. She had called my best friend, Tony Robbins, the Personal Development speaker. He wanted me to come over to his home in San Diego the next night and see him. He insisted on talking with me about what was going on in my life. Lisa said, "You go, or I'm leaving."

I was furious. She had no business calling my friends about me. But she left me no choice. I had to go.

The next night both of us showed at Tony's. To my surprise, he had over seventy people sitting in his living room. It was one of the first of his many seminars entitled "Date with Destiny." A few years later, he would be giving that same presentation in front of 5,000 people. But we were there in the early days of his business.

I thought we were going to talk in his office. Instead, he called me up on stage in front of 70 people and started grilling me. He wanted to know what was important in my life and what meant the most to me. Being a close friend for over 10 years, he knew I felt that my family was important. He was pressing the issue.

I was furious. He was embarrassing me in front of my wife and people I didn't even know. We started to argue and actually started shoving each other. I told him to back off, and he wouldn't. He was beating me up with his questions and accusations. My mind was exploding.

I looked out in the audience and caught Lisa's face. I could see her tears as she watched Tony and me fight for my life. Then I looked closer and saw my five-month-old daughter in her arms. I could feel the point of Tony's questions burying itself into my soul.

"What's important?"

"What do you value?"

And suddenly I knew. I just stood there like a big gorilla. I dropped my hands down to my side. I didn't know what to say. I knew. It was my family.

"You have to make a choice," Tony said. "If it's your family, you have to choose for your family."

You have to choose for your family.

I walked off the stage, grabbed Lisa's hand and walked out of Tony's house. We drove home in silence. I didn't know what to say. I knew I would have to choose.

You have to understand. There were things I loved about my life. I loved the long lunches with clients. I loved boy's nights out till three a.m. I loved several beers while watching "Monday Night Football" with my pals.

But . . .

I loved my wife more. I cherished my children more.

Paul the apostle made a statement in a letter he wrote to some people in Corinth. He said, "When I was a child, I talked like a child, I thought like a child, I reasoned like a child. When I became a man, I put childish ways behind me."

My wife didn't marry a child. She married a man. But I was behaving like an adolescent. In fact, I was thinking and reasoning more like a six-year-old. I needed to choose to put these childish behaviors away.

My life has changed dramatically since that fateful evening. The nights out with the boys just didn't seem to mean as much to me anymore. I still enjoy hanging with my buddies for sporting events sometimes, but these days a big steak is about all I want to handle.

I had to make choices. I wanted desperately for my wife not only to love me, but to also be in love with me. That was my choice. I wanted her head to jerk up when she heard the garage door go up at night because I somehow completed her world. I wanted her to miss me when she was alone at night in bed while I was out of town, because she wanted my arms around her as she fell asleep.

I made my choice, and I've never regretted it.

I chose romance.

Hats off to Grandma

CHAPTER SEVEN

She was a tough lady.

My grandma, Irene Lown, was the executive assistant to the president of Uniroyal Tire Company. In that role, she was a powerful woman in corporate America. She took no back talk from anybody.

She was one of those women who sacrificed their lives for their families. Her husband ran away early, leaving her to raise and support their only child—my mom. She sacrificed her own desires, and as a single parent, she worked full-time so she could support her daughter. The sacrifice continued when her daughter returned home, after a 15-year marriage with my father dissolved, with four children in tow. She took care of all of us.

Irene took the high ground, bought us all a home and

provided for the family, long after her parenting duties were over. She sacrificed retirement cruises around the world and vacations in Maui to put food on the table and coats on our backs. Again, doing the right thing and being loyal to the family, her character never changed.

I was a tough boy. I didn't let anything or anybody get under my skin. But for some reason, she did. It was amazing how this old woman, who wasn't even my mother, could make such an impact on my life.

My grandma affected the way I would live my life forever, not to mention some of the decisions I would make. One thing she said was, "Michael, as you grow up, when you say, 'I will,' and shake a client's hand, that means you must complete the task."

I hear that thought in my head every day of my life. Complete the task. Honor your word, despite the flexibility of legal interpretation. It governs every business deal I have ever made. I have not always been the smartest guy at the table, but I always made good on my obligations. People on the street know that about me. In the end, it's about integrity.

If you want people to work with you over and over again, you have to honor your word. That's why bankruptcy was never an option during some of my early days with my partner, when some of our deals turned sour. We made commitments, and I chose to honor them rather than take the easy way out. Some of those people I owed money to during the lean years are my closest business associates today.

Significantly, my grandma said one non-business thing that also affects me still today. She said, "Michael, when you say 'I do' to a woman, that means you will stay, no matter what."

I was a 17-year old kid when she told me that, but I have never forgotten it. It's funny how that works. It seemed right, and it became a decision that I live by.

It was not something that came naturally. Most of the men in my family have left their marriages. I am one of the few who chose to stay.

It's a decision that needs to be made once and for all. I don't know many marriages that have come easy. The ones that seem easy I actually find boring. Lisa and I discovered a long time ago that we can hate each other's guts for weeks at a time. What nobody ever seems to talk about are the deep relationships that can be cultivated on the other side of those conflicts.

Guys like me are used to getting things pretty much the way we want them. If it's not right, we get it fixed or trade it in or buy a new one. We learn that we can get almost everything we want when we want it. A marriage that has land mines can simply be swapped out for another.

But that's not so if you promise to stay, no matter what. You can talk about romance all you want, but real romance to a woman is a husband who won't leave, who won't threaten her with walking out when things aren't going right. Real romance is the security a husband gives his wife by being larger than both of them, being able to take a hit and not swat back. Real romance isn't a box of candy; it's a husband who chooses to remember.

There is only one really big decision to make when it comes to romance. It's about how big you are going to play.

Promise to stay, no matter what.

Then make sure she knows.

To Move or Not to Move

CHAPTER EIGHT

Several years ago I got a call from some men I was working with. They were re-organizing their executive management and had created a place in their company for me to join them. They wanted me to come on board and handle their real estate acquisitions on a global scale.

It was a big deal, with large guarantees. It would probably mean over half a million a year, which at the time looked pretty nice. Only one drawback. I would have to move from Orange County, California, to Phoenix, Arizona, home of their corporate offices.

They were calling me day and night. All I had to say was yes, and it was done.

I thought long and hard about it. Every instinct in me was

screaming, "Take it." Nice income, great guys, super golf courses. I would be able to keep up with all my toys.

But I couldn't get around the idea of moving my wife and family. It's not that Lisa wasn't a big girl. For years she was a very successful professional in her own right. It's that I had this nagging sense of responsibility. She had invested herself so heavily into her friends, our community, and our church and her parents, who lived nearby. They were very close.

Our kids were growing up, and the school and sports routines were becoming important parts of our life. Of course, I could move to Phoenix in a heartbeat. But I didn't think I could without breaking Lisa's heart. It would never be about the money for my wife. It would always be about family and relationships.

I know what Lisa would have said if I had asked her. She would have said to do what I needed to do. If I would be happy working in Phoenix, then she would go.

But it just didn't seem right. What went through my head was that even though the guarantees seemed great, there really are no guarantees in business. The only guarantee I had for sure was Lisa.

So we didn't go. I said no. And she never knew.

Until now.

The Price of Going First Class

CHAPTER NINE

I've learned a lot of stuff the hard way.

Years ago, I would reward my special clients with lavish getaways. I knew how to do these right.

For example, each year I would take six or seven guys to Maui to wine and dine them. I would buy first class tickets. When we landed, I would have helicopters fly us to our hotels, and we would land on the roof. I would rent out the whole floor for the week. I didn't bother with rental cars. I would have limousines drive us everywhere. We had spas in every room and a private pool to enjoy.

The restaurants loved us. They would remember us from the year before. We always had the biggest tabs. The tip alone would be $500. As expected, we always got great service.

I must admit, I was one fun guy. I would run the bars. Before the week was over, I would spend a small fortune giving these guys a lifetime experience they would never forget.

And it was a pretty good investment. These guys kept me in business the rest of the year.

Sometime around the second day of the trip, my wife would start to call. I would treat her like garbage. It always felt as though she was checking up on me. As it turned out, she had every reason to. By week's end, we were always in a long-distance battle.

Then I would return home. Exhausted from a hard week working and playing with these guys, it took me another whole week to rehab from my business excursion. My home was not a happy place to be.

I remember one trip in particular. When we were out on one of our dinners, I overheard a guy at the next table bragging about beating up his wife. He disgusted me. I wondered how someone who did that could live with himself. What a wimp.

I now realize there is more than one way to beat up your wife.

The business trips I was taking with my friends were an emotional battering to Lisa.

We were going through some challenging times with the business, and here I was out there spending more in one week than most people could live on for a year. I was partying, hanging around guys with questionable characters, and making a hundred poor personal decisions. All the time, my wife was home, managing the affairs of the family, trying to keep things sane.

The funny thing is I actually thought I was doing the right thing. I really believed it was important for the guys to believe I was one of them. It was important to be where they were and doing what they were doing. And then I would come home and want intimacy with my wife.

Real Mr. Romance!

Sometimes I am so ashamed of the stupid things I have done in my past. I look at Lisa and wonder how in the world she has had the patience to stay around and wait for me to grow up.

A wise carpenter once said you can't serve two masters. He said you will either hate the one and love the other, or you will hold on to one and despise the other.

That was my life. I was holding on to my corrupt lifestyle and figuratively beating my wife.

I still know most of those guys; but I don't do the parties anymore.

We still do business. I think they still like me. If they don't, I don't care.

I can't romance my wife if I am serving another master.

Sentimental Journal

CHAPTER TEN

A few years ago Lisa went overseas to Europe with Lindsay, our daughter. It was a big investment of time and money, but we thought it would be invaluable for mom and daughter to have such a special experience together.

I stayed behind with Brooke, who definitely got the short end of that stick.

I tried to make it worth Brooke's while. We went out almost every night for dinner, and I took off early a couple of days. I let her eat all her favorite foods. I tried to treat her like the special daughter she is. I think I did 100 roller coaster rides in three days. I still get nauseous thinking about it.

Right after Lisa left, I found myself thinking how much I missed her. Now it's not my nature to do sentimental things, but I decided I needed to tell her what I felt about her while she was gone. I picked up a blank notebook from the mall and made a journal entry every day she was traveling, telling her what I loved about her and how much I missed her. I also encouraged Brooke to write her feelings as well on the pages immediately following mine. This is all a little out of character for me.

When she came home, I gave it to her.

I'm smiling right now thinking about it.

If I remember right, we put the kids to bed early that night.

The next time your wife goes on a trip, buy a journal.

The Art of Closing the Deal

CHAPTER ELEVEN

By now you've figured out I wasn't always Mr. Romance.

There was a time when I had a hard time seeing myself tied down to one woman for life. I couldn't bring myself to put an end to my adventurous single lifestyle. Lisa and I had gone together for four years, and I was doing pretty well in my business. But she was making clear sounds that if something didn't happen soon, I might be looking for a new potential mate.

I just didn't want to get married. It was as simple as that. I had absolutely no instincts for marriage whatsoever. When we walked into a jewelry store to look at rings, I actually got sick. I told Lisa, after we left our first jeweler, that we had just visited our last jeweler. If she wanted a ring, she would have to get one we had just seen or go find another one on her own, and I would pick it up later. I just couldn't take it.

The thought of actually getting engaged petrified me. I made reservations at a hotel down in San Diego and had a big night planned, but when we arrived I couldn't face it. We went down to the pool, and I was tanked by noon. I almost got in a fight with a guy wearing a Speedo the size of a Band-Aid because he was blocking my sun. I finally stumbled upstairs and passed out on the bed around 3:30 in the afternoon. I shook myself out of my stupor around six and rolled over to see the woman I was going to marry sitting out in the suite watching TV, waiting for me to wake up. I grabbed a quick shower and took her out to eat and proposed, still feeling dizzy from my earlier activities.

The kind of magical evening every girl dreams of.

At my bachelor party, I fell off a table and almost ripped my ear off. Seven stitches one week before my wedding. Was I lucky. Her father was the first to reach me. Her mother hated my guts.

One of my favorite phrases in business is to under-promise and over-deliver. Companies get themselves into trouble by creating large expectations and then ignoring the client once the sale is made. I have made a career out of promising very little and then delivering more that the client expects. It makes me look great. They love me.

It may work in business, but that principle stinks in marriage.

I don't think Lisa had any expectations that I would be sensitive to her when we got married. I might have been the most selfish person she had ever met. I never had a need I didn't meet. I still have no clue why she wanted to marry me.

It was a bad way to start my marriage.

These days, I want her to expect me to be the most loving husband she could have chosen. I want to be the best I can be for her. I don't want my love for her to be a surprise.

I hate it when we are in a group and all the women share their engagement stories. I am ashamed when Lisa tells ours, laughing I'm sure to cover over the tinge of embarrassment. Maybe, as much as any single thing, I wish I could propose to my wife all over again. All too rarely have I given her any sense of how valuable she is to me. For years she has borne my criticisms and complaints instead of radiating from my encouragement and appreciation.

I want my love for my wife to be the stuff of legends.

Who Gets Treated Best?

CHAPTER TWELVE

Sometimes it's the small things that communicate the most.

In my business, the phone rings twelve hours a day. When you live in California, the days seem even longer. If you aren't at your desk by six in the morning, you are behind the East Coast all day. After the East Coast folks are getting ready for bed, you are still taking care of your California clients. It's a merry-go-round that never stops.

The interruptions can kill you. The best thing I ever did was to get administrative help to build a firewall around me so I can get through the day. I will return every call that comes in. But I can't take every call as they come in.

Of course there is Henri, a friend, a multi-millionaire in gold mining and a financier of one of my companies. When

Henri calls, he always gets through. He is important and never has to wait. Beyond that, everybody else has to wait until I have an opening.

Sometimes I will come out of a meeting and there are fifteen pink messages lined up on my desk. Usually one or two stick out. They are Lisa's.

Major mistake.

Somewhere along the line I realized I was treating Henri, a business associate and confidant, better than I was treating my wife. Why would I be buzzed in a meeting to take Henri's call and not be buzzed to take my wife's call? Was I embarrassed to be talking to my wife in front of my associates? Was my work more important than my wife?

Of course I had believed that she was the first in importance, but it was a dropped ball that I hadn't gotten around to picking up. I decided to tell my staff that whenever I was in the office, they were always to buzz me when Lisa called. I would always take her call, no exceptions. If I was in intense negotiations, then my conversation might be brief. But it would give me another chance to connect with her, tell her I love her and re-enforce again how important she is to me. If the client felt at any moment that he was of secondary importance because he had to wait while I talked to my wife, guess what.

He's right.

From One Deal to the Next

CHAPTER THIRTEEN

One of the reasons my work never seems to end is because I keep bringing on new deals. As soon as one project gets figured out, I'm already knee deep into the next one. Things get boring really fast for me. I love the challenge and the hunt. I love the risk. The bigger the upside, however, the bigger the downside.

When I am in the early days of a new venture, I am consumed. It's all I think about. It never occurs to me that I'm doing work. It seems much more like play. I want to do it.

There is a pattern I have noticed about me when I am in the middle of a start-up. Since I am so fully involved, it is hard for me to separate myself mentally from the work. Even though I may force myself home at a reasonable hour, I am still not all there when I walk into the house. I will kiss Lisa, check in with the kids and then quietly slide in front of the computer to check my messages. The cell phone rings and suddenly, in a very real way, I am back at work.

I think that for a long time I rationalized this as necessary for the family, to keep work moving along, to increase the income we could bring into the home. I have only recently begun to understand some of the damage I have been doing to my relationship with my wife.

There are multiple layers to romance. Often my personal busyness interferes with my ability to react and involve myself with the reality of Lisa's world. Whether she is working inside or outside the home, what she is doing is important to our marriage, and I need to be involved.

Somewhere I had to find a switch to turn off between the garage and the kitchen door. When I stepped foot into the house, I was entering a very unique place. Usually I was the last one to return to the nest. There was so much activity going on when I reattached that only a blind man could miss it. Children were going every which way, the phones were ringing, homework was happening, dinner was on, and the dryer was dinging. It was like a small company. Guess what. It wasn't I who was the CEO. It was Lisa.

I had to learn how to get on the same page with her quickly when I came home. I had to become a functioning part of her world as soon as I stepped into the house.

Lots of guys I know come home and act as though they were the only ones working all day. They find a chair near the TV and yell, "Got anything to drink?" They get up when they have eaten and continue to unwind from a day at the office while their wife goes about the rest of the evening, straightening up, finishing dishes, starting bedtimes for the kids, and folding the laundry.

Oh, yeah—and never mind that she has to start work the same time you do in the morning, after she gets the kids off to school.

But you don't want her to work too hard. After all, you do want to have sex before you go to sleep.

Pretty romantic—no wonder you're not getting any.

Figure it out. You start romancing your wife long before you hit the bedroom. Slide into her world and become an active part. Make it clear that her work is as important as yours is.

The first thing I'll do tonight is wash the dishes. It may be one of the only domestic responsibilities I can't screw up. But at least I'm on the team.

I take that back. I'm going to give her a real break and put the kids to bed all by myself.

After all, they do call me Mr. Romance.

You Can Run, but You Can't Hide

CHAPTER FOURTEEN

Want to watch a company spin around in the toilet?

Mess around with its finances.

There are lots of ways to cause confusion. You can start by bringing in less money than you are spending. Add in not paying your bills because you don't have enough money. Sprinkle in hiding the facts about how bad things really are. Then top it off with acting as if you have no financial problems at all.

In no time, people—good employees—will be at each other's throats. Co-workers will feel lied to, cheated, disrespected, and angry. Long-time employees will leave. Friendships will shatter. And it's all because of the mismanagement of money.

It's no surprise that some very good companies destroy themselves because of the way they handle their finances.

I almost blew my marriage up because of the way we handled finances at our home . . . or I should say, the way I mishandled them. It's funny, but it is the same thing as a business. I wasn't bringing in enough dinero to back up our lifestyle. I wasn't paying the bills on time. I wouldn't admit to Lisa how tight things really were. In fact, I acted like we had no problem at all.

Our difficulties were compounded by the fact that I made my money on the commissions from deals. My checks could be very large, but they were never regular. When a check came in I would spend most of the money before I had a chance to pay the bills.

It was not a happy time.

I wanted control of the finances because I thought I could handle them better than Lisa could. I thought I had it all together. I hated talking to creditors, though. That's one thing I didn't want to do. I would have them call my wife. Pretty slick.

Lisa would call me at the office wanting to talk about the money. I would get upset. I mean I would get really upset. I couldn't figure out why she wouldn't quit hounding me. I just wanted her to leave me alone about the money; that is, leave me alone after she had taken all the calls from the people who were mad about not getting paid on time.

The pressure got more and more intense. She wanted to participate in the decisions about our finances. I would not let her. The dam broke the day one of my clients declared bankruptcy. He owed me $250,000 that I realized I would never see. It was money that I was counting on. I was now in official trouble.

I bundled up all the bills and the checkbook, walked into the living room that night and dropped them in Lisa's lap. "I think I have screwed this up as much as one person can," I said. "What do you think you can do with this mess?"

I remember her just staring at the checkbook sitting on top of the stack of bills. You could feel the balance of power hanging in the air. But she didn't move a muscle.

"No way," she said. "It's your mess."

I started to beg. "C'mon, Lisa. I need you to do this for us." I played the "us" card. I felt a need for a strategic shift of attention away from me.

She wouldn't buy it.

"No, Mike. I'm tired of being yelled at. I'm tired of you getting mad at me because you think I'm threatening your manhood. I'm tired of you promising to do things one way with the money and then doing whatever you want to do."

"I won't get mad."

"Yes, you will."

You can talk about romance all you want. Real romance is knowing when to fold your cards with your wife. She could play this hand better than I could. I knew it. She could create a budget, pay the bills, manage the money, and keep our household financially stable. Only one thing stood in her way.

Me.

That was years ago. Today, I regularly yield to Lisa in our finances. It has been one of the great romantic experiences of our life together. For all the millions of dollars I have been responsible for in my own companies, Lisa handles the financial affairs of our home better than I do. Don't get me wrong.

This is a partnership. She prepares a monthly budget and reviews our bills. How they get paid and how our money is spent are decisions we make together. But it starts with Lisa.

It has been one of the greater experiences of our life together.

Besides, I get to sleep with the boss.

Road Trip!

CHAPTER FIFTEEN

It would never occur to me to go years on end without getting our management team together for some rest and relaxation. The benefits that come from climbing outside the work environment with your co-workers are significant. I see relationships heal and new bonds form. I see people appreciate each other in a whole new light. Individuals discuss problems and share opinions away from the pressure of the moment. These "breaks in the action" are invaluable.

So how did we go years without a family vacation? I must have been crazy.

My home is run like a company. We have people in close quarters, real-life management dynamics, job assignments, payroll, acquisitions, building and grounds—the list goes on.

My family—especially Lisa and I—needed those retreats, just like my management team.

We were talking ourselves to sleep more and more over the affairs of the household. It was definitely cramping my bedtime routine, if you get my drift.

I do know, by the way, what happened to our family vacations. I like to do things in big ways. Early on, our vacations were huge events—flying somewhere, big hotel tabs, the works. When we started to reign in some of our spending, I lost interest in doing something that was smaller in scale. I didn't give much thought to the pure value of getting away as a family.

I was talking to my good buddy Lew Webb one day, and he told me about a family camp that he and his family went to every summer in Southern California. I decided to haul the family up into the nearby mountains and try it out.

Nothing about this experience was what I would have picked for my family. We were laughing when we trudged up the trail and saw our lodging. Talk about rustic. We all squeezed into a one-room cabin with one bathroom. The food was average at best. The threadbare facilities were merely good, certainly not the five-star rating I was used to paying for. But it was cheap.

The experience was spectacular. Sometimes you don't know what you've missed until you have found it. The week with my family at the Forest Home Family Camp was something that caught me by surprise.

There is something very special about being completely absorbed into your family. You create space between you and the outside. You listen to your children and your wife and discover them to be quite different people than you remember them to be. Just as important, they get to see you outside of your regular role. It's relaxed and real.

I was talking to Lisa the other day about our vacation plans for the upcoming summer; this will be our fifth year at Forest Home. I asked her what meant the most to her about our experience. I was interested in her answer.

"Michael, the thing that has meant the most to me happened when you came home and said you wanted to do this with us. It wasn't my idea. It was your idea. I loved you very much for making us a priority. I love having the chance to get away from the distractions of the world and reconnect with the man I married."

Do you hear that?

Find a family camp.

Romancing my wife means many things. Making real time for loving my family, and in the process keeping all of our relationships whole and intact, is one of them.

"Talk to Me, Baby"

CHAPTER SIXTEEN

I'll tell you the difference between a good guy who closes deals and someone who is a superstar.

The good guy gets halfway into a deal and hits a simple roadblock. He attempts to navigate through the obstacle and sometimes closes the deal.

The superstar gets halfway through the deal and realizes he has said or done something really stupid that could kill the deal. He might have destroyed any chance of getting the deal done. It is probably dead. At this point the good guy would already be out the door.

Not the superstar. He rebounds, swoops in, and scores. The superstar is invulnerable. He finds a way. He doesn't lose.

Those same abilities translate to the world of romance.

Sometimes the biggest obstacles you must navigate around are those of your own making. You have to be able to clean up your own mess.

When mobile phones first entered the marketplace, I was one of the first boys on the block to have one. Remember how big and bulky they were when they first came out? Mobile phones were a real novelty in those days. When I brought mine home, Lisa was amazed.

"So you can use this anywhere?"

"Yep."

"That's very cool. What's the phone number?" she asked.

I stared at her. "No way."

"What?"

"No way. I'm not giving you the phone number."

"You aren't giving me the phone number? Why not? I'm your wife."

"Sorry, I don't want people calling me. These minutes cost a fortune. Besides it's for business only. You'll be calling me about bringing dinner home and stuff. **No one** is getting this phone number. Forget it."

And for two weeks the subject never came up again. Until, that is, we were driving down Pacific Coast Highway, the top down on a sparkling Tuesday afternoon.

My mobile phone rang.

Lisa looked over at me and her eyes narrowed.

"What's that noise?"

I reached down on the seat and picked up my phone.

"It's my car phone," I said, looking straight ahead, trying to look calm. Inside, I knew this was not a good thing.

"Who could be calling you? I thought nobody knew your number?"

"Gee, I don't know. I'll find out." I reached down and pushed the hands-free loudspeaker button.

"Hello?"

"Hey, Mike. It's Randy Babcook. What time are we teeing off tomorrow?"

Since the possibility exists that young children might be reading this story, it would not be wise to repeat the conversation that ensued. Suffice it to say that driving eighty miles an hour down the coast with one eye on the road, and all the while trying to explain to your wife why your friend has your phone number and she doesn't, is not for the faint of heart. You know that if you say one wrong word you may never see the inside of your bedroom again.

Fortunately, that wasn't the case for me . . . I only slept on the couch for a week! (Even I am not that good.)

Guess who has my cell number on speed dial now?

Don't Get Too Close

CHAPTER SEVENTEEN

There are just some things I hate.

I hate it when men flirt with their friends' wives.

I see it all the time. Some of my friends do it, and I want to break their necks. It drives me crazy.

They walk up to women and give them an extra hard hug or kiss them on the lips. They are the ones who have a million compliments regarding your wife's attractiveness. You know just the ones I'm talking about. It kills me.

When I challenge them on it, I get the same answer every time. "Gee, Mike, that's just how I do it. I'm just a friendly guy."

Right.

It's not just how they do it. They don't do it with women

who aren't attractive. It's always the pretty one that they "just the way I do it" to.

I have had the women they hug tell me they are repulsed when they see these guys coming toward them. They hate being treated like that.

Save it for your own wife, will you?

It's just a matter of time before you get yourself in trouble and look stupid trying to pretend you don't know how it happened.

So if that's just the way you do it, then change the way you do it. I'm telling you here gently.

If I catch you hugging my wife like that, I'll break your arm. Because that's just the way I do it.

The In-Laws

CHAPTER EIGHTEEN

I'm not always the most sensitive guy in the room.

It shouldn't surprise you that the secret to my romantic instincts lies in keeping my ears and eyes open. I learn from other people's success.

One of my close friends has taught me a way to love my wife that I didn't even know existed.

Tom Ketchum is a hard-working, self-made man. He has been successful because he does the little things right. He takes care of his customers and pays attention to details. Clients like Tom.

Tom is just as busy as I am. But Tom finds time to romance his wife by loving her parents. He amazes me.

Tom opens up his home to his wife's mom and dad. He flies them in and personally picks them up from the airport. He calls them on the phone and is involved in their life. He is over the top. It's not because they are his best friends. I know—we've talked about it. It's because he has decided to honor his wife by honoring her parents. And it impresses the heck out of me.

I'm used to guys whining about their in-laws, complaining because their in-laws don't give them money, upset because they are visiting again. I have never seen a husband be as kind and as generous to his wife's parents as Tom is.

I know how much my wife loves her parents. I know this is one thing I can give Lisa that is over the top and unexpected— for me to go out of my way to extend my appreciation to her folks. What a great way to romance my wife.

Thanks, Ketchum. I owe you one.

Who's Getting Treated the Best?

CHAPTER NINETEEN

There are good secretaries, and there are bad secretaries.

I have had both.

The bad secretary makes you want to rip your face off. They are like gasoline on a fire. Give them a project and it instantly becomes ten times bigger than it really is. They require constant personal maintenance and actually make your workload heavier rather than lighter.

The good secretary is a gift from God. Give a project to a good secretary and you never see it again. Crises are handled before they ever reach your door. With a good secretary, you can do the work of five men.

I had a good secretary once that I treated like gold. I knew how valuable she was. I needed to keep her refreshed and rested. I wanted her at the top of her game because I knew she was, in a very real sense, an extension of me. I knew that she would not be rewarded much throughout the course of her day, so I made sure she knew how valuable I thought her work was.

Sometimes I would walk into her office and tell her to leave for the afternoon. Of course, she would resist, but I would insist. We could cover for her. I wanted her to have some time for herself. I knew when she left my office at the end of a hard day, she was returning to her own home where laundry and children were waiting for her. She was going from early morning to late at night. If I didn't take care of her, nobody would.

It wasn't until just a few years ago that I realized I was treating my secretary better than I was treating my wife. Lisa was going from morning to night, just like my secretary did. She was a tireless worker, seldom rewarded for all her efforts. Nobody ever gave her a break from her responsibilities. When my day would end, hers was still going. In fact, it was not uncommon for me to be lying in bed, yelling for Lisa to stop for the night.

And more than my secretary or any person on earth, she extends me.

But who takes care of my wife? Who makes sure she is rewarded for many of the things she does that nobody sees? Who gives her a break and tells her to just leave, that we will cover for her? Who makes sure she is refreshed or even gets one good night's sleep when the kids are up sick with sore throats for a week?

I am not a guy who writes sloppy love letters to his wife. If that's your idea of romance, knock yourself out.

I'm a meat and potatoes guy. I may not send her love notes, but I can start loving her by letting her know she means more to me than my secretary. I need to be the one who makes sure she is rested, gives her breaks from the pressures of the family, and rewards her for her tireless work.

Granted, this is your fundamental Romance 101 stuff. But hey, I'm good at the blocking and tackling.

And there's something I get out of it all too—I've started to realize that my wife needs me.

You see . . . they don't call me Mr. Romance for nothing.

The Backstop

CHAPTER TWENTY

If you work with me, there are certain non-negotiables that I don't budge on.

I expect you to tell me the truth.

I expect you to do what you say.

And I expect you to treat the people around you with respect.

I used to be lax about this last one until a few years ago. I wasn't paying attention to the way we talked to one another around the office. We had a lot of high-powered people running around, in and out, so the language could get a bit short. Sometimes it felt like a college locker room. No thought went unexpressed.

I noticed a pattern that bothered me. Some of the individuals on my team were being openly disrespected—"dissed," as they say on the streets. They were on the short end of the stick when someone got mad. People's feelings were getting trashed. Others in the office began to expect things out of certain individuals without asking. There was no expression of appreciation when something was done. It was beginning to break some of my people down.

I had to put a stop to it.

I first had to admit that I was the main culprit. I expected things out of people when I could just as easily have done it myself. I was often short-tempered. I would very rarely express appreciation for something that was done. Perhaps others were just copying me.

I went to my people one by one and expressed my concern over what was happening around the office. I expressed my commitment to change myself. I also made it clear that if I heard anyone around work disrespecting someone else, they would have to deal with me. That stuff was ending now.

Of course, that was only half my challenge. I needed to be concerned at home that the same thing didn't happen. I could tell my girls all I wanted to about how much I loved their mom, but if they saw me treating her poorly, they would imitate me. I made it clear from the early days with the kids that I was backing Lisa's play. They needed to treat Lisa with respect, or they would meet Dad the wrong way. Not only would I not tolerate disrespectful words, but I would not tolerate the wrong attitude and the wrong tonality. However, I also knew when it was time to step aside and let Lisa exhort her own authority. I couldn't take over for her and still expect the kids to respect her when I would leave.

Don't get me wrong. It was my goal to be a tender and confirming dad, as well as a no-nonsense father. You can't be one without the other. The girls have always known that I am on Mom's team. I am her greatest champion.

The gift of romance is so very deliberate. I don't have to walk into a florist and buy a bucket of flowers to express to Lisa how special she is. I can show her by the kind of language and respect I allow to be directed to her in my home.

And it starts with me.

You're Only as Good...

CHAPTER TWENTY-ONE

It's important to surround myself with good people. It's my personal philosophy to bring individuals around me who are better than I am. It just makes me look good.

We were designing several image pieces for one of my companies recently, and the designers wanted to know what I thought. They wanted to know what I wanted the brochures to look like. "Hey, if I knew that, I wouldn't be writing you such a big check. You are the expert. You tell me what they should look like."

I also surround myself with people who give me good advice. I have boards and investors who are only a phone call away from any input that I need. I even know which guys to call depending on what kind of advice I need. I play to their strengths.

A few months ago, we were in the middle of a search for a COO for one of the companies. I had met a few times with a certain individual that I felt might be a good candidate. It was time to get the reaction from some other people in my circle.

The two of us were sitting in my office, waiting for a board member to come by for lunch when Lisa stopped in. I introduced her to the candidate, and she sat down to talk with us. Soon after, one of my board members, R.C., arrived for lunch and Lisa went on her way.

That night, Lisa and I were lying in bed when Lisa brought up the meeting in my office.

"So, was that the guy you are thinking about hiring as the new COO?"

"Yes. He's one of the candidates."

"Hmmm," she said.

"What?"

"Nothing," she replied.

"Come on. What's with the hmmm? Didn't you like him?"

"Not really. Something drew a red flag that I didn't like."

"How can you know that?" I asked.

"I don't know. It's just my gut. I don't think he's the right guy."

I rolled over, sorry I had even brought it up. Then it occurred to me—she brought it up! So I just mumbled, "I don't know yet. We'll see."

The next day the phone rang in my office. It was R.C., the board member from the lunch the day before.

"Hey, Mike. How did you like that guy yesterday?" he asked.

"First, I'd like to know what you thought," I replied.

"He wasn't the right guy. I don't know what it was, but my gut says he's not the guy," said R.C.

Then I said, "Yeah. That's what I thought. Thanks." I hung up the phone.

I can remember sitting back in my chair and stewing over my conversation with Lisa from the evening before. She had said the same thing. But I had such a different reaction to her than I did to my board member. After all, R.C. is a business leader. Lisa is just my wife. R.C. says, "No" and I say, "Good." Lisa says, "No" and I say, "How would you know?"

It's one of the ways I must continue to stretch myself toward my wife. I must respect her opinion and tell her so. She has shown herself to be on point as least as much as my buddies. I make hundreds of business decisions a day, but I consult my wife on very few of them. I may not go to her with every decision or ask her opinion on every issue, but when I do, I should give her the due she deserves.

It's all part of romancing your wife.

Thanks, Duke

CHAPTER TWENTY-TWO

You get used to being the boss.

Everything revolves around you. You make the final decisions. You make sure you have things the way you want it. Everyone has to work together to please you. If the boss isn't happy, then someone is in trouble.

I admit I have been a lot of boss to deal with. Some of my greatest personal stretching has come from developing sensitivity to those who work for me. Sometimes it not just about me. Sometimes it's needs to be just about them.

It's pretty hard to leave the boss thing at the office. In the evening, the garage door flips up and everyone in the house freezes. The boss is home. When I walk into that house, I naturally think it's all about me. That's the way my whole life is.

But that kind of thinking about kills any hope for real romance.

Luckily for me, I have had help in figuring the way out.

When we had our first daughter, I was still on the me-first automatic pilot. It all began when Lisa went into labor. We checked her into Hoag Hospital in Newport Beach, a wealthy community in Orange County. Everything was five-star. When we took the tour during the birthing classes, I knew this was where I wanted Lisa to have our babies. The birthing rooms were like luxury suites, with large screen TVs, VCRs, stereos, and queen-size beds. I could bunker down in one of these suckers for as long as it would take, no problem.

When Lisa thought she was starting contractions, we checked in around midnight. They slowed up after we got into the room, so a nurse gave her something to help her sleep. I wasn't going anywhere, of course, so I settled in for the night.

Lisa woke up around three in the morning to find me gone. She heard some laughing and my voice outside in the hall. She got up and shuffled to the door. I saw her poke her head out into the hallway. I had ordered pizzas for the midnight shift of nurses, and we were all laughing together, sharing reactions of new dads to the births of their children.

I could see the look on her face from clear down the hall. Lisa needed me. By the time I got to her room, she was already climbing into bed, mumbling under her breath.

"What's the matter? Here, let me help you, Sweetheart."

"Don't worry about me, Mike. I'm just in a mood."

I decided it would be wise if I sat and stayed awhile. Even in a bad mood, I knew she needed me there.

Lisa woke up a little bit later, and we took a little walk around the halls. Her mood didn't improve. She was sure the doctor would send her home to wait some more. We went back to the room, and the doctor came in and decided to break Lisa's water to hurry things along. Lisa told me to go ahead to the office, only a few miles away, as she knew things would be a while. She would call when something happened.

As I was walked into my office, the phone rang. It was Lisa screaming for me to hurry back. She was going into some serious labor.

I hustled back to the hospital and back to my wife's side. I settled into that slow, along-for-the-ride-wait that husbands go through. This time, however, I came prepared.

I had not forgotten that big screen TV from our hospital tour. I knew then that it would come in handy if this turned out to be a long labor.

I reached into a duffel bag and unzipped it. Lisa rolled over to the edge of the bed and looked down to the floor.

"Do you have a surprise for me?" she asked in a tired voice.

"Nope. I have a surprise for me." I pulled out my prize.

I jerked my arm up in the air in triumph. In my right hand were two John Wayne videos, Chisum and Big Jake. In case we had a long stay, I brought two more guy flicks in the duffel bag: The Guns of Navarone and The Dirty Dozen.

"Ha! The Duke and I can wait all day for this baby."

Lisa rolled over and muttered something under her breath. To this day, I don't know what it was.

By the time the second movie, Big Jake, was done, it was

time for Lisa to do her thing. I whispered to Lisa that if it was a boy, I wanted to name him Jake.

Our first child wasn't a boy. When Lindsay was being born, something happened to me. Something changed within me that affects me to this day. While Lisa was giving life to our daughter, I stood and watched. There was no one to block, no one to persuade. There was no one to call, no deal to close. It was all Lisa. And what I saw her do swallowed up forever all the stuff I had done or would ever do. She was more of a man than I would ever be. And for the first time in my life, I understood that it wasn't all about me.

The curtain had just come down on the boss.

While they were cleaning Lisa and the baby up, I walked over to the TV to put the John Wayne videos away. One of the nurses came over and mentioned how nice it was that I had brought some things for my wife to watch. I nodded. I was kicking myself inside. I didn't realize until that moment that the TV was for Lisa. I thought everything was for me.

Someone came in a little while later and asked what Lisa wanted for dinner. The hospital provided a dinner to all new moms from the cafeteria. I told them I would take care of it. I called a French restaurant that Lisa loved and ordered dinner for two and gave them the hospital's address. They told me they didn't deliver. I told them they did now—and don't forget the candles. I made them an offer they couldn't refuse.

Being Mr. Romance has its advantages. One of them is having the guts to make a right out of a wrong. The other is to be married to Mrs. Romance, who keeps letting me get it right.

Of course she's a John Wayne fan. Just ask our dog Jake.

"Listen, Hun..."

CHAPTER TWENTY-THREE

I like people. I want them to know that I like them.

If you are my friend or are on my team, I want you to feel special, taken care of.

I call my secretary by her name. Sometimes, though, I would respond off the cuff and call her "Hun." I didn't mean it as short for Attila; it was short for "Honey." It seems to make sense to me. My secretary was special, and I wanted her to know I saw her that way. So "Hun" was a term of endearment or a passing comment. She took care of me.

I didn't think anything of it.

I should have.

Lisa and I were eating out one evening, and I asked her to pass something to me. I said, "Thanks, Hun," as any normal husband would say.

I could see her stiffen.

"What's wrong?"

"I don't like it when you call me that. Please don't."

I had no idea what I had done wrong. My mistakes are usually much larger than this one seemed to be.

"What? What did I do now?"

"I don't like it when you call me Hun," she said.

I was stunned. "You don't? Since when?"

"Since every time I hear you call your secretary that."

"But I call lots of people Hun."

"That's just my point," she replied as she leaned over. Lisa got very serious. This was going to be something very important, I could tell. I leaned over toward her, because I had a sense I would get one shot to get this right. I needed to hear every word.

"That's why I don't like it. You don't even realize that you are doing it, Michael. It really hurts me to hear you talk to anybody else that way. Those are words that are reserved for me. They make me feel special, like I am special to you. You're talking to me like you talk to your secretary. What's special about that?"

She leaned back in her chair. I could see I had hurt her more than I had ever intended.

"So don't call me that again, please."

I resisted the urge to say, "Sure, Hun." I hated moments like that, because you know instantly what you have to do, but if you do it right away it looks like you are doing it because you were just told. So I just nodded, and went on with the evening.

The next day, on my terms, I whispered in Lisa's ear that she was my only Hun, and no one would hear that term of endearment except her.

Lots of little things go into romancing your wife. Our wives are stronger than the toughest of us men and softer than they would have us know. I'm a busy guy who doesn't have the luxury of waiting for Valentine's Day. If I can show her she's special today by reserving certain words just for her, then I can't do that fast enough.

On Time

CHAPTER TWENTY-FOUR

I think if you asked many of my clients why they liked working with me, they would say it's because I do what I say. If I have a meeting with you at three o'clock, I get there on time. I don't want to be late. If you can't trust me to be on time, how can you trust me with your deal? I'm an old-fashioned guy. My word is my bond.

It took a while for that philosophy to make its way into my relationship with my wife, however. For some reason, I didn't see things the same way at home as I did at work.

After our first daughter was born, Lisa and I were locked in the house for the first several months. Well, as I think back, it was Lisa that was locked in the house. Having a child was a new experience for both of us, and we didn't trust anybody with our daughter. That was a big switch for someone used to going out every weekend. We started to talk about what our first evening away might look like.

I was hanging with a big client at the time, not a guy Lisa thought a whole lot of. He had a lot of energy, and his personal values were quite a bit different from mine. He had just divorced his wife to marry her younger niece—oh, great guy! Marrying his wife's niece. Don't get too close to this fellow.

Of course, Lisa and I received an invitation to a wedding that we thought was more than a little questionable. Lisa didn't really want to go. She doesn't have much respect for guys who run out on their wives. I had only one answer—Palm Springs.

Besides, he was an important client. I needed to be there. This was not at a time in my life when I was ready to make a large personal statement. I was still a one-of-the-boys kind of guy. We went to the wedding.

We were both more than a little concerned about what we were going to do with our infant daughter Lindsay since she was going with us to the wedding. The hotel managed to arrange a babysitter, something we felt funny about. I assured Lisa our daughter would be fine and ushered my nervous wife off to the wedding party. The nuptials were scheduled for 10 p.m., and then there would be a big party. I know that's unusual, but you didn't know my client.

We had a good time for maybe fifteen minutes. Lisa was oblivious to everything that was going on. Soon, she started whispering to me about going back to the hotel.

"You want to go back already? We just got here."

"I know. I'm not enjoying this. I should be back with Lindsay."

It didn't bother me that Lisa wanted to go back to the room. I was feeling a little nervous, too, but since she was making a big deal about it, I didn't want to admit it.

"I'm going back," she said.

I looked around at the party going on all about me.

"Okay. I'll wrap things up here and be ten minutes behind you."

Lisa gave me a quick kiss on the cheek and hustled on back to the nearby hotel.

Almost four hours later, Lisa heard the key turning the lock to the door.

I looked up and squinted. The light from the room seemed very bright.

"Nice ten minutes," she said.

I cleared my throat.

"What time is it?" I asked.

"Well, let's see," she said. "I left just after ten, and now it's after two in the morning. Did you get lost?"

"Umm, well, actually, a little. We were racing golf carts down Bob Hope Drive and couldn't find our way back."

"You were racing golf carts. You said you were right behind me. Where do golf carts fit in?"

"Umm, well, nowhere really. We were just messing around."

"You are always messing around, Michael." Lisa turned around and left me standing in the doorway.

I'll never forget the words she threw over her shoulder at me as she closed the door to the bedroom.

"You would have never done this to a client."

And she was right.

One of the biggest pieces of my romance puzzle was the slow discovery that my wife didn't need me to become something other than I already was. All she needed from me was to be consistent. She would find me very romantic if I just treated her like I treated my clients. I would never tell my client one time and intentionally be late by four hours. The thought of something like that made me shiver. But my wife somehow got outside my focus zone. Tell her one time, be there another. Did it really make a difference?

Yes, it did, and yes it does now.

I'm not late anymore—not if I want to be Mr. Romance.

It's All About
My Space

CHAPTER TWENTY-FIVE

I love it when I walk into a guy's office and he has one of those massive desks with nothing on it except a phone and a pad of paper. He looks like a beauty queen sitting back there, as if he has everything under control because his desk is clean.

What I'm thinking is that he really has nothing going and that his mother got him the job. All he has to do all day is keep his desk tidy. I have this shmoe any way I want him.

Now, come on into my office.

There is stuff happening in there. I have deals over here, and I have products I'm looking at over there, and paperwork waiting to be signed neatly stacked next to the phone. I feel like my office is like the inside of my brain. It's alive.

Many years ago I hired a new secretary who thought she

was doing me a favor by staying late one evening and cleaning my office. When I came in the next day, I can remember standing in the doorway and feeling my knees buckle. Everything was straightened up and put away. Everything was gone.

My desk was wiped clean. There was only a phone and a pad on it. All my deals were filed. In my view, this was the office from hell.

I couldn't move. I felt like my whole life had been wiped clean. The afternoon before, I had known just where everything was. I had six deals going, and each one had been arranged just right on my desk. I had messages and notes positioned just where I had wanted them. All of it, every single piece of paper, was in its right place.

I didn't know what to say. When my secretary arrived for work, she was certain that I would thank her for taking care of my mess. What she didn't understand was that my office was not hers to clean. It was my space.

It wasn't too long after that I got into a little tussle with Lisa at home. My wife has a home office, but her style is a bit different than mine. She has this bad habit of putting things away. Her projects are usually neatly filed. Her office is in pretty good shape. That is, until I walk in.

Lisa will leave the mail stacked up on the desk for me to look through when I get home from work. One day, after I had finished reading the mail and gone off to do other things, Lisa called to me from her office.

"Michael, could you please come in here?"

I walked into her office. Lisa was standing behind her desk.

"Yes?" I was trying to sound preemptively sweet.

Something was about to come down. I know these things.

"Michael, take a look around my office and tell me what you see."

I remember looking around. Nothing seemed out of the ordinary. "Everything looks normal. What?"

Lisa pointed to the day's mail scattered all over her desk. She turned and pointed to crumpled envelopes that had missed the trash can and were lying on the floor.

"Is this the way you found my office when you came in?"

"Um, no."

"Then why do you come in here and mess it up like this? Don't you think this might bother me?"

"I'm sorry. I guess I wasn't thinking," I said.

"Michael, for such a smart guy, you don't think a lot. You do this continually. I'm getting really tired of it. It's not just here. Last night you threw all the leftovers away from the refrigerator. I know you hate leftovers, but the girls and I had food in there that we wanted to eat. You have no consideration for other people's space. You mess things up, and you throw things away that aren't yours. If I pulled these stunts in your office, you would fire me. I don't know how to fire you."

I was surprised at how much energy Lisa was throwing at such a trivial matter. Then I remembered how angry I had been when my office had been straightened up.

She was right. I would never allow someone to treat my space the way I treated hers. I was being the gorilla again.

After almost twenty years of marriage, I am beginning to understand that romance really happens in the trenches. It's woven with all these little things, these tiny considerations, and these small adjustments. So much of romance is grounded in respect and self-control, all things that are within my grasp every day.

Okay. I can handle it. I'll be more careful. It may be the least I can do.

A Promise with a Ring to It

CHAPTER TWENTY-SIX

I had a company that designed "spirit wear" as one of its product lines. I like that stuff—polo shirts and caps and sweaters with a company's logo imprinted on it. Not only was this a good product to sell, but spirit wear was important for my company as well. I felt that wearing shirts with our logo made us feel as though we were on the same page. It made us look like a team.

We were at a particular event one time when one of our people showed up out of "uniform." I walked over to her and asked her whether she wanted me to get her something to wear from one of our company shirts.

"No, that's all right," she said. "I don't want to wear the advertising."

I didn't know what to say.

"You don't want to wear the advertising? What's that supposed to mean?"

"I don't like the clothes. I wouldn't normally wear this stuff. Besides, they're uncomfortable. I don't like the way they feel on my skin."

All I could think of was . . . women!

Back at the office the next day, we had a little discussion about spirit and sacrifice and how she stuck out because everyone except her was wearing a company shirt. It caused people to wonder what her problem was, I said. Besides, I took it personally. I felt that she wasn't committed to the rest of us.

I was upset, but I chose not to do anything about it. (If I could terminate someone for that without being sued, I would have tossed her out that afternoon.)

Not too long after that incident, I was driving with Lisa when she looked over at my hands on the steering wheel.

"Michael, are you ever going to wear your wedding ring again?"

I looked down on my left hand. I had no jewelry on of any kind.

"I don't know," I replied.

"Do you think it might be possible to start wearing it?"

"Come on, Lisa. You know I hate wearing that wedding ring. It's uncomfortable. I don't even wear my old football rings. Besides, I put it in your jewelry box. It's in a safe place."

"When is the last time you had your ring on?"

I thought a moment. "Ten years maybe?"

We drove in silence for a while. I reflected back about my

ring and not wearing it. First it had been a joke, then it had become so normal that I hadn't paid much attention to it anymore. I never wore it. Naturally, people always asked me whether I was married, and I would always make a smart comment, something like, "You must not know me very well." I felt that I didn't need to advertise that I was married.

I had tried wearing my wedding band for two weeks after the marriage. That had been nearly a decade ago.

After a few miles, it was clear that Lisa was deep in thought. I knew I had to go in after her.

"What are you thinking?" I asked.

She turned and looked at me. I could tell she was really troubled. "I am wondering why, after almost ten years of marriage, you are ashamed to let people know that we are married."

Have you ever had a moment in your life when all of a sudden the lights go on, as if someone was lifting the shades up? When I glanced over at Lisa sitting next to me, it was as though the last ten years of my life were sitting next to me. There was Lisa, the woman I'd taken into my arms and said, "I do" with. There was Lisa, the mother of my two precious daughters. There was Lisa, the woman who put up with my garbage, day after day after day. There was Lisa, the woman whom I had built a lifetime together with, the woman I loved more deeply than the day I married her.

There was Lisa, wondering why I was embarrassed to be married to her.

"I am not ashamed of being married to you."

Lisa motioned to my finger. "Then why won't you wear

your ring? I wear your stupid shirts."

It took a couple of weeks to find a jeweler who could sell me a ring that felt comfortable. A month later at our ten-year anniversary, I recommitted to Lisa by putting my new ring on, where it remains to this day.

She reached out and grabbed my left hand and squeezed.

I am a busy guy. Frequently I am running out of the house in the morning while Lisa and the kids are shuffling around trying to get started. Not much time for romance.

But before I leave my bedroom, I take two seconds. I reach out on my dresser and grab my ring and slowly slide it on my finger. Then I look in the mirror. Most mornings I can see Lisa watching me out of the corner of her eye, with the same little smile on her face as the first day I put it on.

Ah yes. Mr. Romance scores again.

Picture This

CHAPTER TWENTY-SEVEN

Some statistics lie.

Some don't.

Almost twenty-eight million people get their hands on pornography every year. Close to one out of every two are married men.

I was one of the two.

When we first got married, I subscribed to Playboy. I didn't think twice about it. Come on, grow up. It's just pictures. Besides, I bought it for the articles, right?

But having Playboy in the house bothered Lisa. At first, her feelings irritated me. I felt that she was too insecure. The more I thought about it, however, the more I became convinced I was out of bounds.

Nobody I knew—that meaning Lisa—could compare to the pictures in these magazines. Those airbrushed beauties didn't even exist except on four-color pieces of glossy paper. Lisa shouldn't be made to feel as though she needed to compete with these women.

But it was more than that.

It was about integrity and honesty and openness. I was used to making hard sacrifices—I had been an athlete, and I understood the rigors of discipline and the importance of self-control. I always knew I was better than my opponent was because I was not afraid to push through pain and to win at any cost. I always knew I had paid a stiffer price on that field of play and that winning cost me more than it did my opponent.

I saw many guys throw in the towel and walk out of their marriages because they weren't willing to pay the price. They had little invested—no self-discipline. They didn't know how to make tough choices. They were sitting ducks for a marriage catastrophe.

That wasn't going to be me. I was determined not to lose at my marriage. I had to be sharp. I had to be on top of my game all the time. My marriage was important to me.

I canceled the subscription.

You want to win at marriage, you'd better cancel yours.

This was one game I could win.

Quiet Time

CHAPTER TWENTY-EIGHT

I am sitting alone in my office.

Listen.

It's quiet. For the first time today, the phone isn't ringing, I'm not being buzzed, and no one is standing in front of my desk. I have nothing to speed read, no hurry-up responses required.

I am loving this moment of aloneness.

When did this happen? You can't make money if you aren't standing at the plate, swinging at the pitch. Since when did I start enjoying sitting in the dugout and looking out over the field?

Last night I went out to dinner with Lisa. We went to a little Mexican restaurant and sat for a while. We talked and ate. When we were finished, we went for a walk and stopped in a jewelry store to look at some bracelets Lisa saw in the window. Imagine that. Me walking into a jewelry store and not freaking out. We took in a movie that went for a couple of hours. Then we went home.

But tonight, I am sitting here in my office, in this moment of quiet, thinking about last evening and about watching Lisa's face while she watched the movie. I hated the movie. It was a chick flick. I wanted to see some action movie where someone gets waxed, but I let her make the choice. So we went to Lisa's movie. As the film began, I just watched Lisa's face instead of watching the movie.

She loved the picture. She laughed and she cried. And she made me think of all the stuff she does during the day that nobody notices: the beds she makes, the phone calls she takes, the trips to school, the making of the lunches, the dashes to the cleaners, the fixing dinner. And at the end of a day, here she is sitting next to me in a movie theater, enjoying herself.

I'm coming to believe that romance is somehow nursed along by these very quiet moments together.

Life may not be so bad from the dugout.

Final Thought

CHAPTER TWENTY-NINE

I can't do this on my own. I simply can't.

That's a hard thing to say for a guy who lived on the streets at fifteen and has fought for every single thing he has ever had. My life has been a struggle. Nothing has come easy.

But in the end, I knew that I wasn't going to finish the game. I didn't have it in me. I don't know whether I ever told anybody that before. My bravado makes me look powerful, and I never lost—I got what I wanted. So I couldn't lose at life!

But I was. I was losing because at age forty, I felt hopeless for the first time. I had reached the mountaintop, but it wasn't what it was cracked up to be. It wasn't just my marriage that was out of sorts. There were people I was having trouble with and business deals that soured. The peace I was looking for wasn't waiting there for me. I had no center, no focus, . . . no hope. I really didn't know where to go for answers. Every time I trusted people, they disappointed me by being just like me.

I was playing in a golf tournament during this time of my most challenging struggle. The tournament committee slotted me with a guy who had too many things together. Guys like him who have life all figured out drove me nuts.

But something he said created a tear in my life that exists to this day, a rip that changed my thinking forever.

He told me about an old Jewish king named Solomon and some of the things he said before he died—a man who wasn't like me at all, a man they called the wisest man in the world.

In his book called Proverbs, Solomon wrote about what's important in life—that's what I was wrestling with. And in Chapter 16 he said something that cut right to my heart: "If a man's ways are pleasing to the Lord, he will make even his enemies to be at peace with him."

Then I knew that it wasn't a business journey I had been on all those years. It wasn't a marriage journey. It certainly wasn't a money journey. It had been a spiritual journey. All along my life had been about me and God. It wasn't about the deal. It wasn't even about Lisa or the kids. It was about me and God and whether, somehow, I was pleasing to Him.

It's a funny thing. In many ways I didn't change a bit that day. I just missed par that afternoon. And I still got mad because I lost—I hate to lose. But some things did change. In many ways I would never be the same again.

For the first time in my life, I had hope.

But that's another story.